We Need to Talk

We Need to Talk

God Speaks to a Modern Girl

SUSAN BRINKMANN, OCDS

Liguori

LIGUORI, MISSOURI

Imprimi Potest:
Harry Grile, CSsR, Provincial
Denver Province, The Redemptorists

Published by Liguori Publications
Liguori, Missouri 63057

To order, call 800-325-9521, or visit liguori.org

Library of Congress Cataloging-in-Publication Data
Brinkmann, Susan.
　We need to talk : God speaks to a modern girl / Susan Brinkmann.—1st ed.
　　p. cm.
　ISBN 978-0-7648-2222-3
　1. Brinkmann, Susan. 2. Catholic Church—United States—Biography. I. Title.
　BX4705.B8464A3 2012
　282.092—dc23
　[B]
　　　　　　　　　　20120114323

Unless noted, Scripture quotations are from the *New Revised Standard Version Bible*, copyright © 1989 National Council of the Churches of Christ in the United States of America. Used by permission. All rights reserved.

Liguori Publications, a nonprofit corporation, is an apostolate of The Redemptorists. To learn more about The Redemptorists, visit Redemptorists.com.

Printed in the United States of America
16 15 14 13 12 / 5 4 3 2 1
First Edition

Contents

Introduction

*At some point in the midst of
my fifty-hour-a-week job and
twenty-hour-a-weekend writing schedule,
God somehow managed to get my attention.*

This story is for all those ordinary people who think a miracle could never happen to them. The "Red Sea" doesn't part for secretaries and waitresses, but only for the few, the chosen, the holy—or so most of us think.

Read on! As impossible as it might sound, a miracle happened to me, and it did so when I was about as holy as Lady Gaga. In fact, I was what you might call a thoroughly modern girl who wore her skirts short, her jeans tight, her hair as platinum as possible, and enough makeup to cover what was nobody's business but mine.

Yes, when that "great river in the sky" parted for me, I was just another cradle Catholic who did the whole parochial school shtick and ended up being about as interested in God as I was in watching a fly crawl up a television screen.

You see, I came of age in the early 1970s, when women gloried in the freedom to pursue any career they wanted while sleeping around and having abortions whenever birth control failed. It all felt so empowering.

Even after my marriage broke up and I was free to roam, I took great pride in living on my own terms. I worked hard, spent every dime on clothes and miscellaneous fashion accessories and dreamed of one day becoming a great writer. "This is who I am," I would tell any man who took an interest in me, "so either accept me for who I am or go elsewhere."

Not that I was a bad person or even half as selfish as I might sound. I sincerely wanted to marry again and raise a family, but deep down inside I was angry and hurting, as any woman would be after being dumped by the love of her life and left near penniless after working him through college and law school. While he moved up the legal ladder, I moved down to a basement apartment and shopped for groceries at the dollar store.

But when I was writing, it all went away: the sorrow, the pain, the injustice. I would slip into another world where I could live through the minds and hearts of my characters.

Someone else in my shoes might have turned to drugs or booze, but not me. Writing was my therapy. It was how I numbed the pain. It was my passion, my great love, my life. No matter how many putdowns and letdowns I suffered, this one bright hope kept me going. Somewhere, deep down inside where God carves his mark on the soul, I just knew that this was my destiny.

At some point in the midst of my fifty-hour-a-week job and twenty-hour-a-weekend writing schedule, God somehow managed to get my attention, although it's still a wonder to me how he did it. If I hadn't written all this down more than twenty years ago, I may never have remembered the way he snuck up on me, so naturally, so softly, so I-can't-believe-this-is-happening-to-me incredibly. It all happened right smack in the middle of my world, in between firing off letters to publishers, working a sales district from Baltimore to Portland, and dating seemingly every commit-o-phobe on the planet.

I found what I wanted, but it was nothing like what I was looking for. At the time, God was the last thing on my mind. I saw him as a severe old man with a long white beard who sat on a throne in the sky and kept tabs on all our sins. He was more like a gargoyle than a God, and the Church he created was full of misogynists who hated women and did everything in their power to keep us barefoot and pregnant.

And, in my opinion, the people who followed him were even worse. They were nothing but a bunch of geeks in thick glasses and bad haircuts who shouted "Praise the Lord!" at inappropriate times and spoke in Bible verses rather than plain English. They were "Jesus freaks," and there was no way I would ever be like them. In fact, I can distinctly remember the time I told God that I would rather kill myself with a butter knife than turn out like one of them.

Having said all this, when you read the contents of this book, you will come to agree that what happened between God and me beginning in late 1991 was nothing short of astonishing. Sure, it's another conversion story, but what makes mine unique is more the way God behaved than the way I did.

He came to me exactly where I was in life. He entered my world, wading into knee-deep piles of sin, slogging through the fog of my politically correct world view and dealing daily with my stubborn refusal to like him. He never once tried to make me into someone I wasn't. He accepted me for who I was and left all the choices up to me.

As incredible as it might seem, in spite of all my resistance and utter unworthiness, he worked a gigantic miracle for me. And it wasn't some happy little moment. It was *huge*. It was the biggest thing that ever happened to me, so big that it changed me—and my life—forever.

This is the story of that miracle, and I'm writing it for everyone who really needs to know that there is a God.

He's not a gargoyle.

And if he'll do all this for someone like me, he'll do it for you, too.

Chapter One

I had absolutely no luck.
Some people were born winners. Not me.
The only thing I ever won in my life was in the
fourth grade when I took first place
in the Fire Prevention Week contest.

"Congratulations! You're going to be married soon!" Lillian exclaimed.

"Really?" I was shocked. "Are you sure?"

"Yes! Yes! And soon!" the psychic declared, delighted with my reaction. "He's going to be very different from you...from a much different background...maybe from another part of the country or a different religious persuasion, or maybe even an unusual ethnic background."

Her voice trailed off as she closed her eyes and slipped into another one of her trance-like states. While she altered her consciousness, I welled up with newfound hope, feeling almost giddy inside. Did I really want to get married this badly?

I was sitting on the edge of my seat now, hoping she'd tell me more about him, like if he was handsome, sensitive, romantic, successful, and loaded to the gills—you know, all the things a modern girl looks for in a man. I didn't think any of these qualifications was too much to ask, especially in light of all the freedom I'd have to give up in order to keep him happy, bear his kids, and hire someone to do the housework.

I decided to clear my throat to jolt her out of her trance. She opened her eyes and chuckled to herself. "You'll never believe this, but I think he's my nephew!"

"Are you kidding me?"

"Yes, that's him." She started rummaging in her handbag. "I have a picture of him in here somewhere."

A moment later she was showing me a picture of a very handsome man, big and dark with expressive eyes—just my type. My hopes soared.

"All right, I'll go out with him. Here's my number," I said a bit too quickly.

I got home, flushed and excited, and called my best friend, Pam, who recommended this particular psychic to me. "You were right about Lillian," I gushed. "She's great! I walked out of there believing that I might finally start having a life."

I went on to tell her everything Lillian predicted, that I'd have three children—two boys and one girl who was not biologically mine—probably the child of this "very different" man I was going to meet who could be her nephew.

I was walking on air for days, especially after talking to Lillian's nephew, Don, for almost two hours on the phone the week before our date. That thrilled me even more. Finally! A man I could actually talk to. We decided to spend our first date in New York City and take a helicopter ride over Manhattan. How romantic!

The night before our date, I got home from work, flipped on the television and listened to the headlines: "...Tourist helicopter crashes on the banks of Manhattan Bay. No survivors."

This could only happen to me.

I had absolutely no luck. Some people were born winners. Not me. The only thing I ever won in my life was in the fourth grade when I took first place in the Fire Prevention Week contest. My prize was a cheap plastic trophy that broke in my book bag on the way home from school.

This helicopter crash *had* to be a bad omen. In spite of how great Don sounded, I had a sinking feeling this was going to be another date from hell.

It was.

He stepped out of the car sporting cowboy boots, Elvis sideburns, and about 100 more pounds than his picture. I knew before I opened the front door that this date was dead-on-arrival.

I tried to be fair and at least give him the benefit of the doubt, but my benevolence ended by the time we reached the Jersey turnpike.

"Did I mention my wives the other night?" he asked.

"Wives? As in plural? How many have you had?"

"Two already and I'm not even thirty. Can you believe it?"

I'm shocked.

"Talk about being down on your luck, huh?"

That makes two of us.

"I promised myself there would never be a third!"

Then why date? If you don't want a relationship, what's the point? Oh I get it. It's the sex you think you're going to get...over my dead body.

"What do you say we skip the helicopter ride," I suggested. "Especially after yesterday's crash. It makes me woozy just thinking about it."

"Woozy, huh? Now that you mention it, you don't look too good."

Thanks.

I decided never to go back to Lillian again, especially not after the way I blew off her nephew. He left thirty-seven messages on my answering machine—without a single callback—before he finally got the message.

A month later, Pam and I were browsing in a New Age bookstore, looking for we-know-not-what-but-its-got-to-be-more-than-this.

Our spiritual searching always seemed to bring us here, to the land of avatars, ascended masters, and spirit guides. We wanted to connect with the universal life force, to let it lift us to a higher state of consciousness where our minds could be infused with a cosmic understanding of other worlds, other beings.

Of course, we had no idea that there was not one shred of evidence for any of this stuff. Not unless you count the kind that comes from either withered old men with long beards in white saris, or self-made mystics like J.Z. Knight, who claims to be channeling a 35,000-year-old warrior named Ramtha, who appeared in her kitchen one day and told her all the secrets of the universe.

Credible proof didn't matter to us at the time. We just wanted something other than the God of the Bible.

We'd been there, done that.

This other stuff was exciting.

"Let's try these crystals," Pam suggested, and held up a box of rocks. "Wow! Check this out! They retain all the energy from everything that ever touches them—humans, the elements, animals. It says this energy can be very healing!"

"Of what?"

"'Mind, body, and spirit,'" she read from the box.

I picked up one of the rocks, hoping to feel some kind of vibration, but it just felt like cold, hard stone. Kind of like the guys I date.

We left without buying them. They were rocks, for God's sake. If rocks could heal, and we lived on a planet full of them, why were we all still suffering?

I was searching—for meaning, hope, a reason. There had to be more to life than rising before dawn every morning, driving to work, working all day to make other people rich, then coming home to eat, take a bath, go to bed, and start it all over again. Give me a break! That's not living. That's existing.

Like Oprah once said, "I really don't think God put you on earth to file invoices. People don't know how to dream anymore!"

Except me. I had a *big* dream. One day, I was going to be a writer. It was one of those things I just knew down to the very fiber of my being, although I could never explain why. But it's been that way ever since the day I picked up a John Jakes novel, read it, and turned to my now ex-husband and announced, "I could write something like this."

Don't ask me where that ever came from. I'd read hundreds of novels in my lifetime, but this time, I couldn't shake the feeling that I was born to write, as if this was my destiny all along and I was just now discovering it.

For months, I couldn't get it off my mind. It became like an obsession. I kept reading and rereading the book, studying the characters, how the plot flowed. I worked at Penn State University at the time and started keeping sheets of paper under my blotter that were full of ideas about what was to become my first novel.

Funny, but at the same time I had an overwhelming urge to return to church. I was raised Catholic and went to parochial schools my entire life, but I'd been away from the sacraments for years. The whole "God thing" just wasn't relevant.

Only once did I actually follow through with the urge to attend Mass, and I felt terribly out of place the minute I walked in the door. I spent the whole Mass sitting in the back pew waiting to be inspired. I wasn't. When it came time for Communion, I knew better than to receive, so I picked up my pocketbook and skulked out the back door like an escaped convict walking past a guard station.

The truth was, I didn't believe in what the Church professed: no sex, no birth control, no abortions.

Are you kidding me?

Fourteen years and three novels later, I was still no closer to being published. All I had to show for those years was a file full of rejection letters. I couldn't even get a letter to the editor published in the local newspaper.

But I did enjoy a few rare moments of triumph. Like the time I met a famous author at a cocktail party at my ex-husband's law school. He was an eccentric-looking, white-haired English professor who had published twenty pieces of nonfiction with Macmillan. A friend introduced me as a struggling writer.

"What do you write?" he asked.

"Fiction."

His face fell. "Oh. That's a tough market. Very tough."

"Tell me about it. Any advice?"

"That depends on how good you are," he said. "If you can write fiction, the sky's the limit. Nonfiction is a publisher's meat and potatoes. Fiction is the gravy. Big money there if you can really write it. Not too many people can write fiction. It's not the kind of thing you can learn in school. Fiction is all imagination. You either have it or you don't."

"My imagination is legendary," I said because it was true. It drove everyone nuts, including me.

It was the kind that always went one step beyond normal. I remember waking up one night and thought I heard a noise in the kitchen. It sounded like a growl, the kind that a big black bear might make. Not only did I convince myself that a bear was in our kitchen, but I swore it was making itself a bologna sandwich with lettuce and mayo. I actually heard it open the refrigerator door, peel off two bologna slices, tear up a few lettuce leaves, open the mayo jar and hunt around in the utensil drawer for a knife to spread it with. All the while I lay in bed, frozen in terror, hoping against hope that the bear would be too full after eating the sandwich to take much interest in me.

"Oh yeah?" the professor laughed in a way that made me wonder if he was half-crocked. The next thing I knew he was pressing a business card into my hand. "I'll tell you what. Send me one page of your novel. That's all. Just one page. That's all I need to read to know if you can really write fiction."

I sent him a page, and he contacted me a week later to tell me I could write fiction.

"Come over to my house next Saturday morning and we'll have a chat about how to get you noticed in the publishing world," he said.

Things this good never happened to me—ever.

Could you hold a moment? I think I'm having a near-death experience.

A week later, I was sitting in his palatial study, listening to him coach me about writing.

"You've got to develop your own style. Learn how to say things your own way. Don't say them like everyone else," he advised, then stopped and stared off into space for a moment, just long enough to make me think this guy might be a little odd. But weren't most brilliant people?

"Don't say the wind is rustling through the trees," he continued. "Say the breezes are sifting through the limbs or something creative like that...."

"How about...'the wind whispered through the willows like faraway music.'"

"Excellent!" he applauded, and smiled very broadly at me just before something caught his eye in the window behind me. He suddenly leaped out of his chair and pointed, "Look! Look!"

"What?" I cried and shot out of my chair.

"There's a squirrel in the swimming pool!" he cried.

What's a creative way of saying, "You're weird?"

But I took his advice and worked very hard developing my style and trying to be different. It must have worked because not long after this I landed an agent. Gerry Wilson was her name, and she really believed in me. She was so encouraging and upbeat, even though her letters were always full of disappointing news.

"Bantam liked your work, Sue, but they've already bought enough fiction this year and aren't looking for anymore," she'd write. "But they loved your work! Everyone who reads you is really impressed with your talent."

Then why doesn't anyone buy it?

My prospects for getting published never seemed to brighten, but I was past the point of giving up. Trying to get published had become a way of life. It was like being on a constant journey, always traveling toward the Promised Land but never quite reaching it. And so I kept plugging away every weekend, always hoping this novel would be "the one."

"Yes, but if you become a writer, what are you going to do about health insurance?" Pam would ask. "Publishers don't provide healthcare, you know. One serious illness—just one—and you're wiped out for life!"

This was a part of her I could never understand. She was so damned practical. How could the need for health insurance override self-fulfillment, a happy life, a reason to be? Was it really that important to get your prescriptions for two bucks?

"Don't kid yourself, Pam. You're paying a lot more for your health insurance than you think. It's costing you your life!"

She hated when I said that, because deep down inside, she knew it was true. She worked for a teachers union, and I never once heard her say how much she loved her job. It was always, "Only eighteen more years before retirement."

Not me. I needed more. And so I kept on dreaming of the day I'd become a writer and life would be worth living. This was why I *never* worked overtime. I left at five bells and didn't think about the place until I arrived the next morning. The object was to save all my brainpower for writing. Even if I had to travel for work, I'd take my novel with me and work on it in the hotel room at night.

Writing was the only thing that felt right to me. In fact, I used to joke with my friends about the profound peace that came over me whenever I was writing, saying it was "like having one long Communion with God."

That was why I was so sure that one day I would make it. One day. Not that my life was a failure. I had a decent job, a company car, an expense account, lots of friends.

No love.

It bugged me. I wanted to settle down with a good man, raise a family and be a writer. Just like that old TV show, *Please Don't Eat the Daisies.* That was my dream, my utopia: a husband, three kids, a shaggy dog and an agent who didn't care how many publishers turned me down.

Instead, I had an ex-husband, two cats, a dozen zebra finches, and three unpublished novels.

At about this time, things started to go bad at work. The owners of the company decided to sell out, and everyone was getting the ax. I would be the last to go because I was the workhorse in the office and everyone knew it.

Besides, I was female so I didn't make as much as the guys. If they had to keep anyone, it might as well be the cheap one. Of course, they never admitted it. No one ever addressed my lousy pay except at review time, when they had no choice. That's when they'd pull out the canned excuses, such as, "Well, it's been a tough year, so raises are going to be slim this year." Or my all-time favorite, "The reason you keep getting passed over for promotions, Sue, is because you're too damned dependable. People just forget you're here after a while."

"Oh, I get it. Why don't I start doing a pole dance on my desk every Friday after throwing my chair through a window. Will that get me noticed?"

"You bet! Forget the chair. Just do the pole dance!"

I've got a better idea. Why don't I just sue you instead?

I decided to keep my mouth shut and give them all the rope they needed to hang themselves into a lawsuit—which they did without any effort at all on my part. They did it all on their own, just by being themselves.

I wasn't the least bit upset about losing my job. I'd already made up my mind that after this job I was never going to work in an office again. It was time to make my dream come true, time to become a writer. It was now or never.

I got laid off on a Friday afternoon in the airport. After saying goodbye to my boss, I turned to walk away with pride and dignity, then tripped over a baggage cart. I sprawled on the floor—in a dress—my handbag flying one way, my briefcase in another. Only about 400 bystanders saw the whole thing.

I got to my feet, made my typical joking remarks, and then walked off with my head held high and my nylons in shreds.

Chapter Two

*It seemed that no matter
what was on my mind during the day,
I'd end up reading something about it
in the Bible that night.
At first I thought it was just a coincidence.*

But the severance was good. Really good. And the lawsuit was moving along very nicely because the company didn't have a leg to stand on. That's when I saw an ad for a psychic in the local newspaper and decided to give her a try. Maybe she'd tell me if I would win or lose in court.

I can't remember her name, so I'll call her Diane. She was a nice woman with a tidy condo in a decent neighborhood and a quaint picket fence out front. I liked the place. It gave me a good feeling when I walked inside. She took one look at me and announced, "You're scared. Your life's a mess."

"Yeah, I know," I said, acting like I wasn't at all frightened by what she'd just said.

"Let's sit down. We'll talk."

She told me nothing about becoming a writer, or anything much about my future. It made me wonder if I was going to die soon. Instead, she told me about a book written by a woman at the turn of the century whose approach to life had totally changed her own. She said the book never left her bookstand. She read some part of it every day. Like a Bible.

I can't remember the name of the book, so I'll call it "Make Miracles Happen." I found it a few days later in a ghoulish-looking New Age bookstore filled with books, wind chimes, and frangipani incense.

I started reading it right away. Although I didn't know it at the time, it was the usual "prosperity Gospel," the kind that cherry-picks Scripture for any verse that makes God sound like he created us for no other reason than to be filthy rich and deliriously happy. If we're not there yet, it's because we don't ask right, the book claimed. Take Jesus at his word! If he said, "Ask and you shall receive," then take him up on it.

OK, I will.

I dog-eared the page, looked out the window and up into the sky and said, "I want to be a writer, get married, have children, and be reasonably well-off."

The writer claimed that if one asked with confidence and true faith, it was only a matter of time before she would start "receiving" whatever she asked for. So why did I suddenly feel guilty, like I'd asked for too much?

Maybe I should drop the "reasonably well-off" part.

Fortunately, the book dealt with such feelings and gave tips on how to retrain our brains into thinking positive about what we deserve. The author recommended repeating different phrases during the day, such as, "Give him a measure and he'll return a treasure!"

I started to do this and, strangely enough, began to feel better about life. I began to think that if I kept this up, whoever I was praying to might just answer. Money was about to come pouring in my windows. I was certain of it. I could sense it, feel it, like something wonderful hovering on my horizon.

You wish.

Weeks passed and no money came. The only thing on my horizon was a date with a man. I met him through a dating service, and he sounded reasonably intelligent on the phone.

"I'm a diamond merchant," he told me.

"Oh, really? What does a diamond merchant do?"

"We buy diamonds from the source and sell them to retailers."

"Where's the source?"

"Diamond mines in Africa."

"I'm not much into diamonds," I said, trying to sound nonplused. "Emeralds are my favorite."

I knew something was wrong with this whole story when he showed up in an old bomb that was filthy inside. I had to push bags of trash out of the way to find somewhere to put my legs.

"Sorry, my ex got the Mercedes," he told me.

Yeah, and my space shuttle is in the shop. A tile fell off in the last reentry.

I wasn't impressed, to say the least, but he did take me to a very fine restaurant. Too bad the hostess sat us smack in the middle of the dining room—the kind of table no one wants. After the waiter took our order, my date reached into his breast pocket, pulled out a white handkerchief and opened it flat. It was full of emeralds.

The people at the next table started gawking. "You want to put that away?" I asked, irritated.

"But I thought you liked emeralds."

"I do, but I'm not into getting mugged on our way to the car."

This guy was nowhere. Not only was he a bald-faced liar, he was walking around with what were probably "hot" jewels in his pockets. If that wasn't bad enough, his breath was foul enough to wilt steel. When we got back to my place, he asked to use the bathroom, and I was terrified that he'd try to kiss me. The mere thought made me gag.

"I have to work tomorrow, so I better get my beauty sleep," I told him the minute he stepped out of the bathroom. It wasn't a lie. I was planning to work on my novel.

"OK, I'm on my way," he said brightly, then leaned down to pet the cat that was sitting on the arm of the sofa. "Hey kitty, kitty," he said, his breath so bad the cat spat at him and ran under the couch.

This one caught on more quickly than Lillian's nephew. After about eighteen unreturned calls, he gave up and left me alone.

It was time to return to "Make Miracles Happen." Maybe I wasn't praying right. Or maybe I was praying to the wrong God. I started wondering who or what I was praying to, if I was really being heard. Was there really a God? When I'd say the prayers recommended in the book, I felt like I was praying into thin air. I didn't hear anyone or feel or sense anything at all. I just felt like I was talking to myself.

Thankfully, the book had a whole chapter dedicated to precisely this problem and gave all kinds of recommendations on how to be quiet and listen to God speak. Get as far away from distractions as possible, it said, even bright lights.

I decided to try praying in my bedroom. I lit a candle, sat in the middle of the bed, turned off all the lights and waited.

Nothing.

Maybe I should stare at the candle flame, sort of like hypnotize myself by watching it flicker.

Then I remembered how I tried to quit smoking through hypnosis, but I never went under. "You're just one of those people who can't be hypnotized," the guy told me.

"Does that mean I get my money back?"

"Well, no!" he huffed indignantly. "I still had to put the time into it."

What about my time? What do I get for sitting through three $50 sessions waiting for you to get the job done?

I put that past failure out of my mind and continued to stare at the candle, hoping something would happen.

It didn't. After a few minutes, I started to get irritated. "This God crap is getting old."

Just then I heard a horrific crash in the living room and ran out to find one of my cats running recklessly through the room, a plastic grocery bag billowing out behind him as he ran. He must have been playing in the bag and got his head stuck in the handle and was running wild trying to get away from it.

"You dumb cat!" I caught him and set him free.

Like a typical non-practicing but still guilt-ridden Catholic, I wondered if the whole episode wasn't God punishing me for saying "God crap" a few minutes earlier.

I went back to staring at the candle and was just starting to feel peaceful, like something might happen, when the phone rang. It was my mother. "I thought you were coming over tonight."

"I never said that."

"Yes, you did."

"No, I didn't."

"Yes, you did!"

I blew out the candle. "I'll be right over, Mom."

For a moment, I stood scratching the melted wax off my yard-sale bargain of a nightstand and wondered what she would say if she saw what I was doing just then, my good old-fashioned Catholic mother.

She'd think I was nuts.

Later, when I got home, I picked up the book again and realized I wasn't so enamored with it anymore. Who was this woman, anyway? Probably the daughter of a tycoon who never had to work a day in her life. "Ask and you shall receive." Ha! I'll bet Jesus didn't even say that!

A Bible.

I wondered if I had one. Not to my knowledge. But I decided to look anyway. Being an avid reader and a writer of historical fiction novels, there were books all over the place, several hundred at least.

Strange, but the first shelf I went to, the first book my hand touched was a Bible.

"Oh, yeah!" I suddenly remembered buying it at a junk shop in Tappahannock, Virginia, because it looked like an antique.

I carried it back to the bedroom, flopped down on the bed and tried to figure out how to use it. Eventually I located the Gospels and the place in Luke where Jesus says, "So I say to you, ask, and it will be given to you; search, and you will find; knock and the door will be opened for you. For everyone who asks receives, and everyone who searches finds, and for everyone who knocks, the door will be opened."

Wow! He really did say that! Maybe I oughta give the book one more chance.

Weeks passed. I continued to read the "Miracles" book and to do my daily chants at night, but I also started flipping through that old Bible. I guess I wanted to know what else he said.

"I will do whatever you ask in my name, so that the Father may be glorified in the Son. If in my name you ask me for anything, I will do it."

I like that kind of talk.

"Take up your cross and follow me."

That part, not so much.

But what I really got hooked on were psalms. They were mesmerizing to a dyed-in-the-wool romantic like myself because every line burned with love.

"I love the Lord because he has heard my voice and my supplications....Therefore I will call on him as long as I live....The Lord is my rock, my fortress, and my deliverer....With my whole heart I seek you....I treasure your word in my heart....You are a hiding-place for me...."

I couldn't help but wonder who this God was that David addressed so beautifully, this God who helped people so much, who was so loyal and loving and *present*.

By comparison, my God seemed more like a vindictive gargoyle, someone who hung around waiting for people to commit sins so he could zap them with lightning bolts. He definitely wasn't someone I'd turn to in everyday life. I'd be too afraid of what he'd ask me to do—like give up drinking, cursing, dating, smoking, living.

After awhile, I actually started to like David's God. He came through in a pinch, like when David's army was overpowered by an enemy and God made all the bad guys kill each other instead of David.

I could use that kind of help.

Before long, I started reading the Bible at night instead of "Make Miracles Happen." In fact, I loaned the latter to Pam to see what she thought.

She didn't get it.

"It sounds too much like the Bible!"

"It's *based* on the Bible."

"Well, I don't want to read the Bible. I don't believe in it."

"Me neither," I lied, and hung up feeling like a Jesus freak.

It was time to stop reading the Bible, I told myself. What would my friends say if they knew? They'd check me into a psych ward.

I put the book back on the shelf—for about a week. Then I started reading it again just for kicks. It seemed that no matter what was on my mind during the day, I'd end up reading something about it in the Bible that night. At first I thought it was just a coincidence.

Like the time I was at a family function and was behaving like my usual crackpot self. On the way home I wondered why I always acted like such a goofball around them. That was the role I always played, the silly dreamer who would never amount to anything, who made people laugh and shake their heads and wonder who my real parents were.

That night I just happened to flip open the Bible to Judges 6:15–16, when the Lord called upon Gideon to save Israel from its enemy.

"I am the least in my family!" Gideon protests. "But I will be with you," the Lord replied.

Now what are the odds of me opening a 1,500-page book to that particular passage between God and someone I could actually relate to?

Or the time I found myself wondering if, by any chance, this Bible stuff was God's way of talking to me. Even if it was, why would he talk to me? That very night I opened to Psalm 149, where David sings, "The LORD takes pleasure in his people."

Then there was the impending court date. I was afraid to confront the men from my old company even though I had been legitimately wronged and my case was quite strong. The night before, I opened the Bible to Isaiah 43:5: "Do not fear, for I am with you...."

Could I get that in writing?

I was eerily calm the next day, and I won the case.

Due to my vow never to work in a 9-to-5 desk job again, I had trained to become an aerobics instructor and had only to pass the dreaded exam before I could go to work. The day of the test, I awoke exhausted from lack of sleep, not a good way to start a day of rigorous exercise in front of judges. Certain I was about to flunk, I chain-smoked the whole way to the test. (Whoever heard of an aerobics instructor who smoked?)

After making it through the first half of the day, I bought myself a big lunch and drove out to a nearby park where I could stuff myself, smoke cigarettes, and pray to David's God.

At the end of the day, I didn't have a good feeling about my performance. That night I opened the Bible to Jeremiah 29:11: "...I know the plans I have for you, says the LORD, plans for your welfare and not for harm."

Does that mean I passed?

A week later, the results came in the mail.

I passed.

My first aerobics audition came a few weeks later. Naturally, I prayed to David's God for help. I really wanted this job. It was the start of a new life for me. I opened the Bible and the first words my eye fell upon were in Isaiah 41:10: "I will uphold you with my... right hand."

I aced the audition and got the job.

Chapter Three

"I think God is talking to me."
Pam let out a hoot of laughter.
"Isn't that what all the serial killers say?"
"Knock it off. I'm serious."

I was starting to like this God stuff.

And then one day, at a family party, niece Jessica announced out of the blue, "I want Aunt Susie to be my confirmation sponsor." Everyone fell silent and looked around at each other, smirking devilishly.

"Jess, Aunt Susie's divorced and hasn't been to church in years," my sister-in-law, Debbie, explained in that bright and happy way of hers.

"I don't care," Jessie said. "I want her to be my sponsor."

She was so adamant, I couldn't resist. "It can't hurt to ask. The worst they can do is say no."

"If you don't get struck by lightning the minute you step in the church," one of my naughty brothers joked.

Very funny.

I found out what parish I was in and spent the next Sunday morning driving around looking for the place, even though it was only a half-mile from my front door. By the time I found it, I was very annoyed and cursing up a blue streak.

Knock it off, girl! You're going into a RECTORY for the first time in twenty years.

I parked the car and walked up the path, all the while trying not to feel as out-of-place as a porn star in a cloister.

"I need to see a priest about becoming a confirmation sponsor," I told the lady at the desk.

She showed me into the office of a big roly-poly Italian priest named Father Alex.

"What can I do for you?"

I told him why I was there. He nodded and opened a desk drawer to pull out a form. "You're in good standing with the Church?"

"Uh...."

He looked up quickly. "You attend the sacraments?"

"Which ones?"

A knowing little sparkle flashed from his eyes, and I got the distinct feeling he knew my exact situation.

"Well, you can't be someone's sponsor if you're not a practicing Catholic," he said and smiled very warmly at me, as if to say he understood. It gave me some courage. At least the guy was going to be cool about it.

"The truth is, I'm divorced and haven't been to Mass in years," I blurted, "but my niece insisted she wants no one else for her confirmation sponsor, and I don't want to disappoint her."

For some reason, I slipped on my saleswoman persona, leaned across the desk and said, "But I'll make a deal with you. If you let me be her sponsor, I'll come back to church."

"You promise?"

"I do."

Are you nuts? You just promised a priest you're going back to church!

"Deal!" he said without batting an eye. A moment later, the signed slip was in my hand. "Have you remarried?"

"Uh, no, I'm still working on it."

"Then you might want to consider an annulment at some point in the future." He handed me some forms and stood up. "See you next Sunday!"

I drove off wondering what I had just done: promising a priest I would go back to church. What was wrong with me? I'm Catholic, for crying out loud.

This promise is going to guilt you to death, girl!

It did.

The very next Sunday I woke up and decided, "I'm not going."

An hour later, I was sprawled on the sofa, doing my nails, and thinking, "I don't *have* to go."

By the following hour, it was, "I don't even know what time the Masses are!"

At 12:30 p.m. I was sitting in the back pew feeling like an idiot. "I can't believe I'm here!"

Just then, the choir started singing.

"...Long have I waited for your coming home to me and living deeply our new life." Now why would this just happen to be the first song I heard in a church in twenty years?

I suddenly felt a little choked up, like the way I sometimes did when I read the Bible at night. Why did the words sound so much like something David's God would say?

Get a grip. It's a coincidence.

"OK," I prayed on my way out of the parking lot. "I'll come back, but I'm just sitting in the back row and watching. I'm not getting involved any further. You're not making me into some kind of Jesus freak. I absolutely *will not* go there! I'd rather be dead."

Months went by and I kept my promise, going to Mass every Sunday and sitting in the very last pew. I usually spent the entire Mass thinking about the novel I was writing and stringing together all kinds of creative sentences in my head until it was time to go home.

But a Mass rarely went by without something catching my attention, a phrase in a song, or something the priest said during the homily that connected perfectly with what was going on in my life.

Like the time I was fretting about becoming a Jesus freak and worrying that in exchange for his friendship—which I was really starting to enjoy—I would have to stand on street corners shouting, "Repent! Repent! The end is near!"

A split second after this thought went through my head, the lector read from Isaiah 41:1–2, "...Here is my servant, my chosen.... He will not cry or lift up his voice, or make it heard in the street."

Now what are the odds of *that* happening? This kind of thing happened all the time now, and I must admit it was starting to freak me out. Like the morning I was curling my hair in the bathroom and listening to the morning news. In the back of my mind, I thought about the annulment and wondered what the heck I did with all the papers the priest gave me. Maybe I ought to fill them out, get the ball rolling.

But I was dragging my feet because, to be honest, I thought the whole annulment thing was nothing but a moneymaking racket. It was probably just the usual Catholic guilt that made me think I ought to do it because the priest said so.

But where the heck did I put those papers?

While rolling my hair, my eye kept straying to a certain bookshelf in the living room—and one book in particular. It took a few minutes, but eventually it occurred to me that maybe the papers were in that book.

Nah. It couldn't be.

I started walking into the living room.

But if they are, I'll know there's a God.

The papers were in the book, serving as a bookmark. I suddenly remembered that I had been reading that book when I got the papers and must have stuck them in there and forgot about them.

"Pam, I need to talk to you."

"About what?"

"I think God is talking to me."

She let out a hoot of laughter. "Isn't that what all the serial killers say?"

"Knock it off. I'm serious."

"Will you stop reading those books? You're starting to get weird."

"I'm serious. I really think God is talking to me."

"You're cracking up," she said, then sighed the way she always did. "Go ahead. Tell me the rest of it."

I told her everything that had been going on with the Bible (but not that I was reading it every night), the Mass, the annulment papers. When it was all done, I was shocked at what she said.

"You know, I used to pray a lot when I was a little girl. My best friend used to pray over me and lay her hands on me."

"You're kidding."

"No, I'm serious. One day she laid her hands on me and invoked the Holy Spirit. I had such a feeling go through me—like goose bumps from my head to my toes."

"Yeah! I got that feeling before, too!"

"It was awesome. It was like flying without leaving the ground. It was the greatest feeling I ever had in my life, and I never forgot it. But I went home that day and told my mom and she started laughing at me. I was so ashamed that I never let her pray over me again."

"That's so sad! Why did she laugh?"

"I don't know, she just did. But I think you're right. There really is a God. And I think it was him that day...the real God. You know, the one who loves us."

"You never told me any of this before."

"Guess it never came up." She paused for a moment. "Strange, but I haven't remembered that story in years. I wonder if he's trying to tell me something."

"Like what?"

"Like maybe if my mom hadn't laughed at me that day, I might have become another Mother Teresa."

Now *that* was funny. We laughed until we cried.

Chapter Four

"You know, I'm more than just a body, Paul,"
I told my current boyfriend
the next time I saw him.
"Why don't we ever go out anywhere?"

"Wives, be subject to your husbands as you are to the Lord," the lector read one Sunday from Ephesians 5:22, and I could feel the heat creeping up the side of my neck.

"For the husband is the head of the wife," he continued in verses 23–24, "just as Christ is the head of the church....Just as the church is subject to Christ, so also wives ought to be, in everything, to their husbands."

What a crock!

I was so angry I spent the whole Mass trying to calm down.

"You know, this is the part about you that I can't stand!" I railed at God on the way out of the parking lot. "Why is your Church so draconian about stuff like this? Is this what you really want, for women to be chattel, used and abused?"

I was a dyed-in-the-wool women's libber, a product of the 1960s, when the originals ran around burning bras on national television. They were my heroines. They taught me that women deserved to be treated as nothing less than the equals of men—or maybe even a little better than that—and if we didn't want to get pregnant, that was our business.

And so we ran ourselves into the ground working full time while raising our families and fighting for equality in a patriarchal society that was run by a bunch of couch potatoes who never did their share of anything except drink beer, watch sports, and demand sex.

I was still a little miffed when I picked up the Bible that night for my daily conversation with David's God. Still stewing over the same reading, I decided to read it again and was just about to launch into a new tirade about how the Lord should quit treating women like a pile of menstruous rags when I read something that made the words stick in my throat.

It was the rest of the passage, the part I tuned out because I was too angry to listen that morning.

Right after the part where women are essentially told to behave like butt-kissers, verses 25 and 28 change the subject entirely.

"Husbands, love your wives, just as Christ loved the church and gave himself up for her....In the same way, husbands should love their wives as they do their own bodies."

My anger was somewhat defused by that line, but I wasn't ready to give in yet. It was nice to know the Lord expected husbands to do something in return, but they weren't being asked to serve the way we were. There was something very demeaning about that.

But the wind was already going out of my sails because this sounded more like something David's God would say. He was always fair and never said anything even remotely negative, at least not to me. When we had our "chats" at night, which I guess you could call prayer, every Bible verse seemed to build me up, encourage me, heal me in all those deep inner places where life had left me so weak and wounded. I just couldn't imagine him telling a woman, "Kiss this guy's butt."

A few days later, I decided to check into this whole matter of the Church and its teaching about women and did something I had never done before: read a Church document.

My first choice was *Mulieris Dignitatem*, "On the Dignity and Vocation of Women," by Pope John Paul II, because that seemed to be the most on-point.

I couldn't put it down.

Both man and woman are human beings to an equal degree,

both are created in God's image, the document explained. And because God has both feminine and masculine qualities, men and women are equal images of him.

Believe it or not, this was the first real explanation I'd ever heard about why men and women were equal. Until then, the only reason I knew was "because we are, you Neanderthal!"

The document went on to explain that when we say man is created in the image and likeness of God, this also means that man exists for others. This applies to every human being, whether woman or man.

So that means if we're both equal and both are called to exist "for" others, then when a man is told to "love his wife as Christ loves the Church," he's being called to give of himself in service just as the wife is when she's asked to "serve."

I can live with that.

Furthermore, the document states, "the woman cannot become the 'object' of 'domination' and male 'possession.'"

Apparently, Jesus doesn't approve of this kind of treatment either. What I never knew before reading this document was that Jesus caused quite a scandal in his day by allowing women to accompany and befriend him. This simply wasn't done in that day and age.

In fact, the document says he was a "promoter" of women's true dignity, and this behavior caused wonder, surprise, and even scandal to his contemporaries.

But the best part of the whole document was the pope's commentary on the story of the woman who was caught in adultery.

Jesus says: "Let him who is without sin among you be the first to throw a stone at her" (*MD* 13, and see John 8:3–11).

As John Paul explains, what Jesus is doing here is evoking an awareness of sin in the men who are accusing her, seeing through their hypocrisy, and saying—in essence—that this woman's sin is, after all, a confirmation of their own transgressions, of their misdeeds and male injustice.

That's telling them, Jesus!

The pope says this episode in the Gospel of John has been repeated in countless similar situations in every period of history.

How often is a woman left alone, exposed to public opinion with "her sin" while the man who was equally responsible for that sin walks away scot-free? And yet no one pays attention to his sin, the pope says. It's just passed over in silence. Even worse, sometimes a man will actually make himself the accuser, such as in the case of the woman caught in adultery.

Sometimes?

The woman not only pays for her sin, but his, too, the pope says, and she does so all alone. How often is she abandoned in her pregnancy when the child's father is simply unwilling to accept responsibility for it? And because of the pressures faced by so many unwed mothers, how many of them resort to abortion? They get rid of the child, but at what price? the pope asks. Even more poignant, he goes on to say that although society likes to whitewash abortion by calling it a choice rather than the sin of murder, a woman's conscience never lets her forget that she has taken the life of her own child.

This guy really gets it.

Jesus then directs each man to look within himself to see whether the woman entrusted to him as a sister in humanity, as a spouse, has not become an object of adultery in his heart, to see whether or not she has become an object to him—an object of pleasure and exploitation.

To say I was blown away by all this would be an understatement. I felt strangely vindicated.

"You know, I'm more than just a body, Paul," I told my current boyfriend the next time I saw him. "Why don't we ever go out anywhere? All we ever do is go to your house or mine and fool around."

"But I thought you liked it!"

"It's not about liking. It's about how we never share anything, our interests, our dreams. We're human beings, not animals, for crying out loud."

"Ah! I get it! You're fishing for a commitment."

"I never said that! Why does it always have to be about you?"

He rolled his eyes, then gave me that lopsided little grin that I always found so adorable. "Knock it off, will you?"

I lost the argument that night, and my boyfriend got his way—again.

Later that night, I sat on the edge of the bed, staring at the Bible, too afraid to pick it up and see what God had to say. I was ashamed of myself for not respecting my own dignity and self-worth. I had betrayed myself.

It was only after sitting there for awhile, longing for his company, that I finally picked up the Bible. But instead of scanning the concordance the way I liked to do, I just flipped it open to wherever.

The first line my eye fell upon was from Jeremiah 31:3: "I have loved you with an everlasting love; therefore I have continued my faithfulness to you." I got that choked-up feeling again, the way I always did when I felt the Lord was speaking to me.

But this couldn't be the right reading. Surely he's going to scold me, tell me I have to repent, let me know how disappointed he was in my behavior. I flipped it open again, this time to the eighth chapter of the Gospel of John: the story of the woman caught in adultery.

There was no need to read the story. I already knew it by heart. Once again, I got that choked-up feeling and suddenly felt like that woman who was caught in adultery and left alone in her sin while the man got off scot-free. Yes, I was wrong to behave as I had done, but so was Paul. And Jesus was well aware of that. The blame wasn't all mine.

I could almost hear him saying to me what he had said to that woman centuries ago. "...From now on, sin no more," as Jesus in quoted in the *Revised Standard Version*.

This has to be God, I told myself. Who else could convict a person of sin and make you feel like the most beloved person on the planet at the same time? Only a being capable of unconditional love. This was definitely a much higher love than I encountered in my living room. These men didn't love me. They loved themselves and were only using me to get whatever pleasure or emotional high they needed. I guess I always knew that, but not as clearly as I did in that moment.

But it was also a bit disconcerting because it wasn't at all what I expected God to say. He was supposed to condemn me, tell me how bad I was, how I'd have to live in a tent and eat dirt for twenty years to make it all up to him.

"Why don't you ever say what I expect you to say?" I asked the thin air, feeling strangely upset inside all of a sudden. Maybe I was still clinging to this gargoyle of a God who only existed in my imagination because I wasn't quite ready to open myself up to a God I actually liked.

"Why don't you just be who you're supposed to be! Why don't you just....Oh, forget it! I'm sick of all this God stuff. I'm going to bed!"

I started crying and slamming around the apartment getting ready for bed. Even the cats darted out of my way.

"I've had enough of all this Bible crap," I announced as I slid into bed and punched out the lights.

I'm not going to change, I decided. I don't care if my whole idea about God, the Church, life, is being turned on its head by this... this *being*...who I can't even see or hear.

What am I, nuts?

"I'm not talking to you anymore," I told the darkness around me. "No more. I'm going back to the way I was before...before I met *you*!"

My resolve lasted about four minutes before I started to wonder what he was thinking; if I'd hurt his feelings; what life would be like without him.

"I'm sorry," I peeped and hoped it would be OK.

I got that strange, soft little choked-up feeling that often happened when I was praying, something I affectionately referred to as a "hug" from God.

It felt so good just then it made me cry. I laid there in the dark, quietly weeping and wondering if this is what it felt like to crack up.

Chapter Five

*I began to wonder if I was having
a nervous breakdown,
but I didn't think it could feel this good.*

God and I became a twosome after that, but only he and I knew about it. I kept this part of my life secret, even from Pam.

While I continued to attend all the Sunday-afternoon football parties—where we sat around drinking beer and dropping the F-bomb every time a player did something stupid—my relationship with God began to flourish. I talked to him all the time now, not just during prayer. And I decided the time had come to get another book, something not as intense as the Bible.

I went to a store in a neighboring town called The Catholic Shop. As I pulled into the parking lot, I clearly remembered the last time I was there, with my mom and my sister to pick up a first Communion gift for one of the kids. "Gee Mom, I hope we beat the crowds," I'd cracked. "We might not find a parking spot!" I could still hear my sister and me laughing uproariously.

Remembering that now made me feel even more uncomfortable about walking into this store, not because I had to buy a gift for someone else but because I wanted to buy something for me.

Naturally I wore a trench coat and sunglasses so no one would recognize me. The place was a maze of statues and holy cards and a stereo system playing an instrumental version of "Here I Am, Lord."

Too bad my sunglasses were so dark I kept banging into things, but I finally found my way into a gigantic room full of books. I flipped through the titles until I found what looked like the perfect subject: *Talking to God*. I paid for it and slid out the back door like something out of *It Takes a Thief*.

The book was great. I read the whole thing in two hours. Whether I realized it or not, I had begun a prayer life that wasn't at all what I expected. It was comforting, peaceful and, believe it or not, fascinating. The more I read about God, the more enchanted I became by him.

Contrary to the gargoyle God I had once worshiped, David's God was right up my alley. He supported family life and had a special affinity for the helpless and downtrodden.

Me, too.

He hated suffering, sorrow, and tears.

Gimme five.

And he was willing to die for those he loved.

Better you than me.

OK, so I wasn't Mother Teresa yet, but I was having a wonderful time collecting unemployment, teaching at the gym, watching the Gulf War on CNN, and learning about God.

I should have known it wouldn't last.

That terrible day arrived unexpectedly, and when it did, I realized within seconds that this was the mother of all disasters.

My agent *hated* my new book. She sent it back with a three-page letter outlining all of the problems with it. To say I was crushed would be an understatement. I wanted to throw myself off a ten-story building. This could not have come at a worse time because now I *had* to get published. I had no job and didn't want one. I despised working in an office and just didn't want to live like that any longer.

For God's sake, I'm thirty-five years old already! When is my life going to begin?

For the first time in years, I began to question how much longer I could go on hoping to be a writer, rearranging my whole life around work that had yet to earn me a nickel. My baby brother had a house, a new baby, and a brand-new car in the driveway while I was still living in a basement apartment and driving a clunker with bald tires.

Maybe it was all the years of sacrifice that began to weigh on me, the fourteen long years of chasing a dream that only seemed to get further away. Was it all just a foolish folly that was finally playing itself out?

Maybe this was why I was running out of ideas for another novel—something that had never happened to me before. I never finished a novel without knowing exactly what I was going to write next. Not this time. In fact, the novel I had sent to Gerry was actually an earlier book that I reworked, hoping to improve it. From the sounds of her letter, I only made it worse. Deep down inside, I was really frightened. What would become of me without my dream? I sat on the floor of the study, cradling the rejected manuscript in my arms and bawling all over it. Frightened, sad, angry, I railed at life, the world, me, God.

"Why did you give me this talent?" I said and shook my fist at him. "I always knew it was from you. I knew it from the very start! So why did you give it to me…to torture me with it? What good is a writing talent if I can't do anything with it?!"

Enraged, I threw the book across the room and glared at the heavens.

"Are you for real?! I mean, is all this God stuff really true?! Because if it is, and you're listening, I need help. If you don't help me get published, then give me cancer," I declared dramatically. "You might as well just kill me."

After a long time, I got up and took a bath. Even though I was still angry inside, I was a bit concerned about having spoken to God so disrespectfully just then—and to ask to die, no less! Thankfully it was winter, so the chances of being struck by lightning were pretty slim. Still, I stayed away from the windows just in case.

For a long time I laid on the bed in a state of utter despair. I was almost too drained to open the Bible, but something made me pick up the book and flip it open to the concordance to see what topic might be germane to someone who was experiencing the end of the world as she knew it.

Funny, but the name "Philadelphia" caught my eye. Because it's near my hometown, I flipped open to Revelation 3:8, the place where the angel is reading a letter to the Church in Philadelphia.

"I know your works. Look, I have set before you an open door, which no one is able to shut," I read as a flood of goose bumps rushed all over me, from head to toe. "I know that you have but little power, and yet you have kept my word and have not denied my name."

The goose bumps suddenly seemed to explode across my skin, so powerful now they felt almost like an electric shock. I had never felt *anything* like it before. These things were downright nuclear. They were so intense it felt as if my body was being physically lifted off the bed. In fact, I actually looked down to be sure I wasn't levitating, that's how strong it was. It was terrifying, but thrilling at the same time. For a long moment I just hung there wondering what to do: stay or run for my life.

"I have set before you an open door...." Could this mean what I thought it meant?

No, it couldn't be. Nothing this good ever happened to me.

I threw the Bible down and ran out of the room.

This is too weird.

I had a sudden, overwhelming desire to do something normal—like the dishes.

What the heck just happened to me?

Somewhere deep inside I knew it was momentous, whatever it was. God heard my prayer, and those nuclear goose bumps were from him. I just knew it. He seemed to be saying that he was going to "set an open door" before me.

Could that be the door to Doubleday, Lord?

Whatever happened to me that night I still can't explain, but life was never the same again. I was suddenly, inexplicably joyful. And I had never felt so positive about getting published in my life. I went from a state of complete despair to unflinching hope in a split second. It was as if my whole life had changed, even though nothing changed. I was still unemployed, unpublished, and out of ideas.

I began to wonder if I was having a nervous breakdown, but I didn't think it could feel this good. I was *soaring.* Every time I read that passage (which I did at least four times a day) I became more convinced that God was up to something. He was going to open the door that had been shut to me all my life.

So how is this going to happen, Lord? And could it happen sometime between today and tomorrow?

Out of nowhere, I suddenly felt this driving compulsion to dig up a novel I had written ten years earlier. Oddly enough, it was titled *Divine Origin.* It took me awhile, but I finally found it and started reading it over the Christmas holidays.

By mid-January, I was rewriting it.

The work went amazingly well. It was the best writing I'd ever done—smooth and fluid and full of heart. At the end of the day, I'd read over what I had written and would marvel at the uncanny beauty of it. I had never written like that before. Even more strange is that there were often whole paragraphs that I honestly could not remember writing.

I began to make jokes about it to Pam. "I think a dead writer is writing through me." I finished the book on Holy Saturday of that year, said a prayer, and sent it off to my agent.

The next day, Easter Sunday, I was walking on air. The joy I felt inside was so intense it has been permanently imbedded in my memory. It was all I could do to contain myself while celebrating the holiday with my family. No way could I let it show. I could just hear my brothers tease: "What're you so happy about? What's his name?"

"Jesus! And he's going to get me published!"

Yeah, right. Excuse me while I slip into this straitjacket.

Whether it made sense or not, I was literally bubbling over with excitement. I had no black-and-white confirmations, but I just knew that something was going to happen this time. This was not going to be just another rejected book.

A month later, I received a glowing review of the book from Gerry. "Sue, I think you finally got it right this time," she wrote. It was just the confirmation I needed to bolster my faith that God was really working on my behalf. Gerry said she was sending the manuscript off to an editor at "a major publishing house" with no corrections needed.

Weeks went by, and when I didn't hear anything further, I started to worry. Surely the editor would have contacted Gerry by now if she liked it. Doubts began to creep into my heaven. The only thing that held me together now was a parade of "minor miracles" that kept me hoping against hope.

For instance, my annulment papers had been submitted, but

I still owed $350 for processing. I had no idea where the money would come from—until one day when I opened my mail to find a check from the IRS. Apparently I had overpaid my taxes the previous year by a total of $348!

Another time my car broke down in the middle of an intersection during a torrential downpour. Two men were kind enough to push me off the road, but there I sat, waiting for the rain to stop so I could walk to the nearest gas station. Finally, a middle-aged man pulled up in a car that had a backseat full of Bibles and offered me a lift to the nearest gas station. I remember thinking to myself, *How bad could he be with all these Bibles in the car?* I got in the car and he drove me to the only gas station on the planet with "Praise the Lord" on its marquee.

We both got out of the car, and I just assumed he was following me inside to help me explain what was wrong with the car. But when I turned around, he was gone without a trace. There was no sign of him—or his car.

"Where'd he go?" I asked the mechanic.

"Who?" he asked, and looked at me strangely.

"The guy who just dropped me off."

"Here?"

"Never mind," I said and hoped he didn't see all the hair on my arms stand up.

But most times it was just little things, such as when I'd have to lead a class at the gym when I was feeling under-the-weather. I'd ask God for help and end up teaching a class that left them drowning in their own sweat.

"Wow!" they'd say later. "What did you do, get a B-12 shot?"

"Heck no," I'd reply. "I rely on a higher power."

If they only knew.

As the weeks droned on and I still heard nothing from Gerry, clouds started to obscure my sunny skies.

You're so desperate for a life, you're making all this up about God... and now you've convinced yourself it's true. You're under too much stress. You've finally lost it!

One night on the way home from the gym, I was having one of these anxiety attacks when God decided to set me straight. It happened while I was battling my doubts by recounting all the minor miracles God had been working for me when suddenly, out of nowhere, a crystal-clear thought ran through my head. "If I can work all these little miracles for you, what makes you think I can't work a big one?"

There was a strangely commanding quality about the thought. "Well, I guess you can," I stammered aloud. Just then, I got those nuclear goose bumps again and my throat closed up with an unexplained surge of emotion. It was so strong it brought tears to my eyes and a desperate cry out of my heart.

"Don't let me make this up, OK? It means too much to me. It's my dream, my life. It's all I have!"

I cried the rest of the way home.

Chapter Six

"You know, Father,
maybe I ought to tell you what I didn't do,
otherwise we'll be here all night!"

"This suit is challenging five regulations in the Pennsylvania Abortion Control Act," said the anchor on the nightly news, "such as a requirement that a woman tell her husband before having an abortion."

I shot out of my seat. "Are you kidding me? Ask her husband's permission? For what?"

The television screen filled with angry pro-life protestors carrying signs that read, "Abortion is Murder!" and I felt my blood pressure rise.

"Abortion is *not* murder! It's a blob of cells, for crying out loud. What's wrong with these people?"

OK, I was coming back to the Lord, but I still had a long way to go, and the whole abortion battle was one of those areas that continued to make no sense to me. Most abortions were done early in the first trimester, when the "baby" was just a blob of cells. It didn't even look human yet. At most, it looked like a human head with a long tail attached.

Besides, I thought that if abortion wasn't legal, what choice would women have who found themselves pregnant at an inopportune moment in their lives: the back alley or a coat hanger? How many more women would have to die before we stopped making this unfortunate but necessary procedure into a one-way ticket to hell?

I prayed for guidance, but that was before I knew to be careful what you pray for. The guidance came all right, but it was nothing momentous, nothing that would have caused me to change my mind on a dime. Instead, it came in this little trickle of "facts" that slowly blew a hole in my every right-to-choose argument, forcing me to confront how gullible I had been to the feminist spin machine.

For instance, I just happened to turn on the TV during a show on advances in ultrasound where it showed a ten-week-old baby with fingers and toes and a heart that had been beating since the second or third week of her life. This was obviously more than a blob, and because most abortions took place around this time, I was a lot more disturbed by the thought of subjecting this tiny person to being ripped out of the womb via vacuum aspiration.

Something (or should I say someone?) made me look into this a bit further, and I only uncovered more troubling facts, such as how every medical school textbook in the country taught that life began at conception. The only people who said otherwise seemed to be those involved in the abortion industry. Their bottom line depended on lulling women's consciences to sleep by telling them their babies were just blobs and not fully human yet, so they weren't actually killing someone when they had an abortion.

And we bought it hook, line, and sinker. At least I did. So what did that make me? A brainless automaton, that's what. This was embarrassing—at first—but it quickly became infuriating. Like when I discovered that the famous "coat hanger" argument was nothing more than a colossal myth used by pro-abortion groups to manipulate the public. According to the medical journals, women had stopped dying from back-alley abortions decades before Roe v. Wade with the discovery of penicillin. In 1941, abortion-related deaths were at 1,400. By 1966, they at 120.

Even more galling, I learned that Planned Parenthood, one of the biggest purveyors of this myth, knew all along that it was a bald-faced lie. In the July 1960 edition of the *American Journal of*

Public Health, an article by the medical director of Planned Parenthood, Dr. Mary Calderon, stated that ninety percent of abortions are done by physicians.

"Call them what you will, abortionists or anything else, they are still physicians, trained as such. They must do a pretty good job if the death rate is as low as it is," she gushed. "According to her, abortion—whether therapeutic or illegal—is, in the main, no longer dangerous, because it is being done well by physicians."

Is that so? You lying broad! Women like that should be put in jail. The least they can do is tell the truth to their own peers instead of making us all look like a bunch of idiots who get their facts from the back of a cereal box.

Because the Casey v. Planned Parenthood of Southeastern Pennsylvania abortion case was all over the news at the time, it didn't take long for all this to come up in conversation.

"Men have absolutely no say in what we do with our bodies," a coworker said one day when a bunch of us were out to lunch. "That needs to be codified and put into the Constitution."

"Fat chance," another sneered. "As long as men are running the country, they'll only write laws that suit themselves. If they do away with Roe v. Wade, we're all in trouble! We'll be back to dying in back alleys."

"That's not true," I said and they all looked up sharply, then hung on my every word as I explained what I had discovered.

"Are you kidding me?" one coworker asked when I was finished. "That's really bad. I mean, why would they do that?"

"To make the public more willing to allow abortion?" I asked, and shrugged. "I don't really know, except that they're apparently as political as the men they despise."

Everyone fell silent and went back to eating—except the most outspoken feminist among us. She looked at me like I was some kind of heretic.

"So what are you, anti-abortion now?"

"No, I'm anti-lying," I quipped. She didn't say anything, just went back to eating.

But there was still one other issue that bothered me. I could understand why we weren't allowed to have abortions, but the Church outlawed birth control, too. They might not preach "barefoot and pregnant," but weren't these teachings giving women no other choice?

I decided it was time to sit down and read that infamous document no one paid any attention to—except to mock—the one I'd spent half my adult life laughing at even though I had never read a single word of it.

Humanae Vitae.

Once again, I barely got off the first page when I realized this was going to be another *Mulieris Dignitatem.* Every word made the most brilliant sense to a libber (although now somewhat of a shaken one) like me who believed she deserved much better from the men in her life.

Apparently, the Church feels much the same way. As it turns out, she's not against controlling the number of births, only against the use of artificial means to do so. Why? Because this turns the sexual act into something used merely for self-gratification rather than for the purpose for which it was intended, to unite a man and woman in love and to create children. By doing this, it undermined marriages, families, and women in particular.

Was it possible that the Church's position could sound so much more romantic than the world's? But what really made me sit up and listen was reading the four prophecies the pope made about what would happen to the world if birth control came into widespread use. Every single prophecy had come true in the course of my lifetime. Such as how the use of birth control would lead to marital infidelity and a general lowering of moral standards. Who could argue with that one? Nearly half of all marriages now ended in divorce, and sixty-two percent of American teens had sex before graduating high school. Before the advent of the pill, the number of sexually active teens barely registered on the radar screen.

He also warned about what could happen when the power of preventing birth fell into the hands of the state and women were forced to use it. Who hasn't heard about China's draconian "one-child only" policy where women pregnant with a second child are herded up like cattle, strapped to a table and forced to have an abortion. The pill was barely fifty years old and already half of all world governments had "family planning" programs.

Leaving the creation of life up to people bodes only ill, the pope says, and will lead to crossing boundaries that shouldn't be crossed, such as cloning humans, experimenting on embryos, creating chimeras out of a mix of human and animal genes.

But the one that really got me was the prediction that the use of birth control will make a man forget the reverence due to a woman and reduce her to being a mere instrument of pleasure rather than treat her as a partner who should be graced with loving care.

In other words, the pill makes her into a sex object—exactly what we libbers were trying *not* to be.

To say I was chastened by all this would be an understatement. This changed me. These were some of my most deeply held beliefs: that women deserved to be the masters of their own bodies who should be able to get abortions and take the pill and tell the old-fashioned Roman Catholic Church to get with the program.

But I was wrong about all of it, and for a long time I felt uncomfortable in my own skin, like I didn't recognize myself. I could suddenly understand opposing arguments the way I never could before, and for a long time I felt awkward around people, like I didn't know how to respond. This was a whole new point of view, and it took a while to process it. Oh, I still believed that women were equal to men, but I was coming to that conclusion by a much different route. My dignity had been redefined. It was on God's terms now, not the world's.

It wasn't long after this that I decided to quit taking the pill. "I flushed my birth control pills down the toilet this week, Paul. I'm not taking them anymore."

He looked like someone just hit him in the groin.

"What?"

"You heard me. I'm done with all that."

"But why?"

"For several reasons," I began with great confidence because I'd been practicing all week. "First, I've been taking them too long and want to stop for awhile to let my body take a breather. Second, I don't like the way being on the pill affects my relationships. It makes men think of me as a sex object rather than a person."

He just stood there staring at me in utter disbelief. "But what are we going to do now?" he asked, obviously incapable of seeing my needs through the haze of his own.

"How about having a real relationship instead of just fooling around all the time?"

This suggestion went straight over his head.

"Come on," I said. "Dinner's ready and I got us a movie for later."

For the remainder of the night, he was distant and preoccupied, and when he left, I had a sneaky feeling I'd never see him again.

I was right. After months of dating every weekend, he just disappeared into thin air. Sure, I was hurt, but I wasn't stupid enough to think I'd lost a relationship, because Paul and I never had one. We had the same kind of relationship everyone else had these days —with men wanting it to be all physical and noncommittal and women either pretending they agreed or bamboozling themselves into believing that being used as a sex object was somehow liberating. Were we that desperate or just that dumb?

It was time to start accepting the new me and forget about that old girl whose rule of life was built on a bunch of feminist fairy tales. But I wanted to make a clean break, which is why I decided it was time to go to confession. I'd been putting it off for a long time, ever since my last confession fifteen years ago when the priest chewed me out. I could remember it like it was yesterday.

"Father, I missed Mass last Sunday."

"Why?"

"Because I was out too late the night before and couldn't get up."

"Oh sure! But you weren't too tired to go out, were you?"

What? Are you for real?

"Excuse me?"

"You heard me, young lady!" he said in a voice that was loud enough to pierce the seal on the confessional door, if you know what I mean. "You have time for partying, but when it comes time for God, you're too tired."

I never said that!

"Father, I am truly sorry."

"Well, sorry's not good enough."

For Jesus, it is! Ever hear of forgiving seventy times seven?

"What are you going to do about it?" he demanded.

"Try to do better?"

"Yes well, we'll see, won't we?"

No, because I'm never coming back here again, you old fart. Who needs this crap, anyway?

When I opened the door of the confessional, people standing in line craned their necks to see who just got her butt chewed out by the priest. Talk about embarrassment!

But that was then, and this was now. Strange, but I wanted to go even in spite of that bad experience and the fact that David's God never said anything to guilt me into it. He just didn't operate that way. This was totally my choice. I knew what his commandments were just as clearly as I knew I had been breaking them. And I just didn't want to hurt him. He was so good to me, so tender and affirming, always giving me hope, joy. Everyone else laughed at me when I spoke about becoming a writer, but not David's God. He always took my side and treated my dreams with respect.

It was the least I could do for such a priceless friend.

I called the rectory and made an appointment with Father Alex for the following night. To say I was nervous would be an understatement. I was cold nearly to the point of paralysis and could barely feel my feet as I approached the rectory door.

Father Alex was smiling as usual and motioned me into a chair on the other side of his desk. We exchanged pleasantries, and I could only hope my mouth didn't sound as dry as it felt.

For a few minutes, I tried to calm myself by yucking it up. "You know, Father, maybe I ought to tell you what I didn't do, otherwise we'll be here all night!"

He thought that was real funny and laughed so hard it made his whole belly shake. "I'm not going anywhere," he said brightly. "So why don't you start by telling me the last time you went to confession."

"Fifteen years ago. The priest jumped down my throat, so I never went back."

He shook his head like he'd heard this a thousand times before. "OK, why don't you tell me what's on your heart—the one that bothers you the most—and we'll move on from there."

That sounded like a good plan. I took a deep breath and gushed out the worst of my sins. I was too ashamed to look at him.

"OK, what else?" he asked as if I just told him what I had for breakfast.

"Did you hear what I said?"

"Heard you just fine. Go on."

I told him everything I could think of, things I hadn't remembered in years. The drugs, the men, the booze, the lies, the psychics, palm readers and astrologers. Everything. I felt sorry for this poor priest and the way I was spilling my guts all over him, but there was never the slightest hint of any shock or disdain on his face as I rattled on and on. I could have kissed him for that.

I even confessed the time I asked God to either get me published or give me cancer. "I really feel bad about that," I said.

Father Alex just smiled and said, "Don't worry about it. That was probably the first time you ever really prayed."

I hadn't thought of it that way before. "Yeah, but what about all the times when I'm praying and I refer to the Blessed Trinity as 'you guys'." I could see him choke back a laugh. "I don't mean to. It just comes out that way. Isn't that irreverent?"

"Yes, but oftentimes when God first reveals himself to people, he does so in the way they most need him. And right now, it sounds like you just need a friend, someone to take your side."

You got that right.

When I couldn't think of anything else to confess, I stopped, took a deep sigh, and felt suddenly great inside—like a huge weight had just been lifted off my heart—or was that my soul?

Father Alex grinned happily. "That was a really good confession, Sue. And you know why? Because you told it like it is. You didn't make all kinds of excuses or blame anyone else. You admitted your mistakes and accepted the blame for them. God couldn't ask for more from you right now. Now make your act of contrition."

I drew a blank. For the life of me, I couldn't remember the prayer. After a very long moment, I was forced to admit, "I can't remember how to say it." Feeling like an idiot, I suggested, "Could I just say it in my own words?"

"That's even better," Father Alex said.

This guy should be pope.

A moment later, I was telling David's God how much he meant to me, and how sorry I was for living my life as if he didn't exist, and for all the lousy things I'd done during that time.

Out of the corner of my eye, I watched the priest's hand rise into the air and his voice whisper softly, "With the authority of the Church, I absolve you from your sins...."

A moment later, he was showing me to the door. "Now go home and have a nice dinner," he said.

To this day, I remember exactly what I had for dinner that night: spaghetti and meatballs. It was the best spaghetti I ever ate. Everything tasted better, looked better, felt better. Because *I* was better. If people with a sick soul could be healed, I imagined they would feel just like this—light and airy and happy inside—in some deep, deep place where the essence of oneself is found.

Every time I thought about the confession, I would choke up and cry. There I sat on the living room couch, a mouth full of spaghetti, sobbing.

After all this, you finally cracked up.

The next Sunday I went to Communion for the first time in twenty years, and there are no words to describe that fabulous moment when I finally made physical contact with David's God. In my mind there flashed a picture of the Blessed Trinity, the Father sitting on a throne, Jesus standing beside him, and the Holy Spirit hovering above.

Out of the depths of my heart, I blurted, "You know, I'm really starting to love you guys."

I started crying and struggled so hard to contain myself I almost burst all the blood vessels in my neck.

"Mommy, what's wrong with that lady," the little boy next to me whispered.

"Don't stare," his mother reproved.

It was the happiest moment of my life.

Chapter Seven

Believing in Satan was a little too backward for me. I considered myself more sophisticated than that.

Jim was such a nice guy. He was clean-cut and godly and treated me like a person rather than a toy. If only he hadn't made that *huge* mistake on our first date!

We planned to go out dancing, but not the kind you do in a bar. This was real ballroom dancing, which was being offered at a local church hall. We thought it would be fun and arranged for him to pick me up at 7 o'clock the following Friday evening.

He barely showed up and introduced himself when he asked, "May I use your bathroom?"

"Oh sure!" I said brightly and showed him the way. He was in there for a long time, long enough that I took my coat off and sat down for awhile. When the door finally opened and he came out, the foul odor that wafted into the living room nearly bowled me over. Now what kind of guy shows up for a first date and does *that* in the bathroom? He couldn't take care of *that* before he got here? Good grief. The least he could do was light a match. No matter how gentlemanly he behaved while escorting me out of the apartment, I was completely turned off before we even got to the car.

The dancing was fun, but it was hot in the hall and my hair started to droop. Jim was a great dancer and had a handsome smile and was interesting to talk to, but he did *that* in the bathroom before we left, and I just couldn't get over it.

When we left the hall, I just wanted to go home, but he suggested we visit some friends of his who lived nearby.

They were nice people, but they were watching a Bible story on TV, and all of a sudden one of them hooted, "Praise the Lord," so suddenly that I jumped in my seat and spilled half a glass of soda down the front of my really expensive, fashionable, and therefore dry-clean-only outfit.

Now I was really annoyed. First *that*, then this hootenanny with a bunch of Jesus freaks.

Lord, I'd rather end it all with a butter knife than turn out like these people.

Needless to say, this date went nowhere, just like all the others.

"I'm beginning to wonder if we're ever going to get married again," Pam whined as we sat alone and dateless on New Year's Eve. Instead of going out, the two of us bought junk food and *Bride Magazine* and sat on the phone planning our second weddings. "Between all those jerks you meet and my man, who has been telling me every week for ten years that he's leaving his wife, maybe we oughta forget it and go it alone."

"Maybe we should. Life would be a lot less complicated without men, wouldn't it?"

"Yeah, but then we'd have to pay to get things fixed around the house," she reminded me.

"You're right. I guess they're good for something. But there are some good guys in the world, in spite of the fact that we never seem to meet any. The only guy I ever really liked since my husband was Paul. He was a good time."

Pam let out a wail of laughter. "Paul? He was commit-o-phobic."

"I know, but we had a lot in common," I insisted.

"Like what?"

"We were both insecure."

She spit out a mouthful of beer. "That's not a good thing to have in common, Sue!"

"It's better than nothing!"

To be quite honest, I didn't care so much about getting married anymore. All I cared about was hearing from Gerry about the book. Any day now, the phone was going to ring and it would be her telling me the good news: that one of the great publishing houses in New York had just offered me a contract for my first book.

So why wasn't the phone ringing? Why didn't I hear from her?

As time went on, those anxiety attacks got worse, especially if I let myself consider the reasons why I thought I'd be getting published soon—because I believed God said so even though I had not one stitch of tangible proof. What if I made all this up? After all, I had the most notorious imagination on the planet. If it could imagine a bear in the kitchen making a bologna sandwich, it could imagine that God was telling me he wanted to get me published.

In fact, it was because of this wild imagination that I made a deal with God right from the start of this rather unusual relationship of ours. If he wanted me to pray to him, he'd have to protect me from making things up because I was such a hopeless case when it came to imagination.

I was certain he agreed, but there was nothing tangible about that deal, either. I was just trusting that he would protect me from myself. What if I just thought he made that deal with me? What if I really was making all this up just like I made up the bear in the kitchen? These were the times when I felt like Saint Peter, who leaped out of the boat to walk on water with Jesus, then looked down and sank.

That was me.

And sometimes when I looked down, it was blacker than hell. The darkest and most despairing thoughts would take hold of me with such power that it was sometimes impossible to shake them and I'd sink into a state of complete depression, which was very unlike me. I was usually upbeat, hopeful, always sure my big break was right around the corner.

It was as if some kind of dark force would take hold of me and whisper in my ear: "You made this all up. Gerry's not going to call. The editor she had in mind didn't like the book. You're going to have to go back to a desk job soon."

One night I was in the grips of this "darkness," and nothing I read in the Bible seemed to address it. I went to bed feeling hopeless, deflated. At some point during the night I woke up and felt so despondent it was actually palpable, as if something heavy was on my back, pinning me to the mattress.

"You oughta just end it now," I started to think to myself, even though I didn't want those thoughts and tried to chase them away. "Nothing's ever going to change. Ten years from now, you'll still be waiting for the phone to ring."

I sank deeper into despair.

The thought crossed my mind that I could get into the car right now and ride up to Old Hollow Road and drive myself off the cliff and into the quarry.

No, it's not quick enough, and it'll hurt too much when I hit the bottom. Why am I thinking about this? Why am I even considering this?

I started praying to God to help me get rid of these thoughts. "Father! Help me!"

Nothing.

"Jesus! Help me!"

Nothing.

"Holy Spirit! Come to my aid!"

Nothing.

"Blessed Mother! Help me!"

Nothing.

"Saint Joseph, help me!"

All of a sudden, behind my closed eyes, I saw a flash of brown wool, the kind of attire I always imagined Saint Joseph wearing. In the same instant, all the darkness left: the heaviness, the negative thoughts, the suicidal ideation. It all vanished so quickly, so completely, it was as if it had never been there. I was astonished at how thoroughly my mood changed from gloomy-to-the-point-of-wanting-to-die to wondering what I had been so upset about.

I bought a book about Saint Joseph the next day and slept with it under my pillow for a long, long time. Then one day I noticed that the prayer section contained a litany to Saint Joseph in which he was referred to as the "terror of demons." Is that what had happened that night? Was I under attack from the devil and Saint Joseph chased him away?

I had read enough to know that attacks such as the one I experienced could come from Satan, but I wasn't yet convinced that he existed. Believing in Satan was a little too backward for me. I considered myself more sophisticated than that. Devils were something people invented so they had someone to blame other than themselves for their transgressions, right?

Oh sure, the popes have tried to warn people over the years, but who listens to the pope anymore?

In the 1970s, Pope Paul VI caused an international incident by warning people about Satan.

We have to realize that we face an evil that is a person, he had said. We know this dark and disturbing being truly exists and is still active, predatory, and cunning. He is the hidden enemy. He finds the open door and comes in.

The press vilified Paul, saying he was going back to the Dark Ages. I must admit, even though I was a nonbeliever in the devil, that last part gave me the willies because it rang true. The devil knew where I was vulnerable—in my dream of becoming a writer and my fear that I was just imagining how God was going to intervene and make it all happen for me. The devil knew exactly how to work on my head to convince me to quit hoping, which was the equivalent of withdrawing the feeding tube from a sick patient.

This dream was all I had, and he knew it.

I remember going to sleep that night wondering about all the things I'd read about Satan, particularly the signs of his presence, which was pretty much anything negative such as dark thoughts, anxiety, fear, anger, impurity. God's presence was marked by the exact opposite—peace, hope, love—all the things I felt when I was praying to David's God.

Yes, I knew all this, but I still wasn't convinced.

I eventually fell asleep, and in my dreams I was back home in my parents' house, in my old bed. It was the middle of the night and all was dark and quiet.

Suddenly, from very far away, I heard the sound of footsteps, very soft and quiet, as if the person was deliberately trying not to make noise by walking on tiptoes. The footsteps walked from the living room and into the kitchen.

It was the middle of the night. Everyone was asleep. There shouldn't be anyone in the kitchen.

The first wave of fear swept over me.

The footsteps were now approaching my door, getting closer and closer. I was really scared now, lying very tight and still on the edge of the bed, listening in a kind of terrified disbelief as the footsteps moved closer to my bedroom door.

The knob turned.

"Oh dear God, help me!" my mind screamed.

Just then, something told me to shut my eyes and keep them closed. It wasn't a voice, just a thought so compelling I instantly obeyed.

The knob turned until the latch clicked and the door began to open. Even before the smell reached my nostrils, I immediately sensed the foulness in whatever was standing on the other side of the door. It was an animal of some kind; cold and dirty and smelling like a damp basement after a storm.

It paused in the open doorway, not three feet away from my head, and was staring at me. I could feel its eyes boring into me with a pitch-black rage. Whatever this thing was, it absolutely hated me.

It stepped into the room and was now standing so close to the bed I could have touched it. I swore it could hear my heart pounding in my ears and making a loud sucking sound with each beat.

"Don't move," I heard in my mind. "Don't open your eyes." This was actually quite easy to do because I truly believed my very life depended upon not opening my eyes, and no force on earth could have made me open them in that moment.

Just then, the figure turned and started walking ever so slowly around the bed until it came to the other side. Once again it paused with its eyes fixed on me, boring its hatred into my back.

Ever so slowly, the mattress behind me dipped as the figure slid into bed beside me. I was now a frozen block of terror. From somewhere in the back of my mind came the realization of who this was. The devil. It had to be. What else could be this evil?

It was lying right behind me now, only inches away, and I could feel the scream welling up in my throat. Something touched my back, and it exploded out of my mouth in one long, bloodcurdling scream.

I suddenly found myself sitting up in bed in my apartment.

Alone.

It was just a dream! A dream!

Dear God! Thank you, thank you, thank you for letting this be just a dream!

And just then a single word went through my mind with the same compelling quality I had experienced in the dream.

"Satan."

The relief froze in my throat.

From that moment on, I believed.

Chapter Eight

Oh my God,
there IS a God.

July 23rd was a rainy day. I can't remember much else about it except that it was completely normal. The same get-up-go-to-work-and-come-home kind of day. As usual, I walked in the door, kicked off my shoes and hit the flashing red light on the answering machine.

"Sue? This is Gerry. Call me as soon as you get this message. Harper just made an offer on your book and I think you should take it. Call me right away."

For a moment, it was as if my senses disappeared. I couldn't think, hear, see, feel. All I remember was staring at the wall across the room and saying out loud, "God, I think I see your face."

I have no idea why I said that. Maybe what I was trying to say was, "I knew you were going to do this! I've been waiting for months! I knew you were there! I knew you were for real! You're real! You're real! And you did this *for me!*"

I collapsed to my knees and knelt there for God only knows how long, gasping, "Oh my God, it happened! It really happened!"

And God did it!

That thought made me shoot to my feet, grab the keys and head straight for church. God must have known I was coming because the door wasn't locked the way it usually was. The minute I stepped into the empty church and looked at the tabernacle, I got those nuclear goose bumps, the ones that run from the top of your head to the tip of your toes and make you feel like you ought to be levitating. This time it was so powerful it made my ears ring and my head feel like it was going to explode.

I was choking and crying now, rushing up the aisle and hoping against all hope that no one would come into the church and make me have to explain all this.

I needed to be with him. Alone.

For the longest time, I sat in a pew and stared at the tabernacle as if seeing it for the first time. God was real. All of this was real. The God, the Church, the angels and saints and devils. All of it. Real.

Oh my God, there IS a God.

"You did this," I choked out loud. "You made this happen for me! I just know it!" I started to thank him but the gratitude I felt just then was beyond words. It was more like an internal tsunami of the deepest and most profound gratitude I had ever felt in my life, and it just gushed out of me in one long, keening sound. There were no words to describe how grateful I was. There would never be words to describe it.

I'll love you for this forever.

It took a long time for me to calm down and get my arms around what had just happened, even though a part of me still felt as if this was happening to someone else and I was just watching it all.

HarperCollins Publishers—one of the "great gray ladies"—one of the biggest publishing houses on the planet—was going to publish my novel!

Someone pinch me.

Even more thrilling was the realization that all this God stuff was true. There really is a God—David's God. This is the kind of thing he would do: make your lifelong dream come true. He was that kind of tender and thoughtful.

I'm never going to forget this, Lord. Never.

Somehow I managed to stumble my way out of church, muttering all the way, "I'm never going to get over this."

I drove home and called Gerry. The more I listened to her, the more real it became. Contracts, royalties, print dates, mass markets, book reviews. She kept saying, "I don't expect you to understand all this," which was a good thing because I was still too dazed to absorb anything she was saying.

"It's not the best contract I've ever seen, but an unpublished author like you needs the kind of 'street cred' you're going to get from being published by a giant like Harper," she said.

My head was spinning.

Maybe I'm having a near-death experience. No wonder people don't want to come back.

"Just send me the contract and tell me where to sign," I said, and she laughed happily.

The first person I called was my sister.

"Are you kidding me?" she gasped. "It's about time!"

You can say that again!

Mom was just as breathless. "You're kidding!" she kept saying over and over as I told her all the juicy details.

The first words out of Pam's mouth were: "After all those years of you trying and everyone laughing at you—except me, of course—now I know there's a God! Only he could pull off a revenge this sweet!"

I couldn't have said it better myself.

"You mean I actually know a published author?" my brother, Rick, said. "I don't believe it!"

My dad called me from the office. "I just want you to know how proud of you I am."

I called everyone I knew and amidst a hundred cries of disbelief, I couldn't stop thinking, *Yeah, but this all happened because I started praying to God a while ago.*

No one would believe me, except Pam. She kind of believed me. "You know, you may be on to something after all," she admitted after I told her the whole story.

On to something? This is cataclysmic! Like the earth turning on a new axis! This is a major paradigm shift. We're not talking about New Age rocks here, my friend. This is *God*, for crying out loud. You know, the one who can part the Red Sea, turn sticks into serpents, and make blind men see.

Forget the New Age. The old one works just fine!

Dazed, bewildered, excited beyond belief, I decided to do something ordinary in order to settle myself down. I went grocery shopping. It calmed me. On the way home, I stopped in to see my mom, who made me eat something even though my stomach was as hard and tight as those knots that form in old sneaker laces.

I told her the whole story, about how I started praying and how God spoke to me and that I'd returned to the sacraments and to the Church. Mom looked a little pained when I told her that because I guess she wanted to believe that I'd never left. Oh well. She kept saying over and over, "You're kidding....You're kidding...."

"Ma, this is no joke. This is what happened. Maybe you don't believe me."

"Oh I believe you!" she said at once, and I knew that she did. "But no one else will. You better not tell this to anyone but me."

"Yeah, you're right."

But I knew that wouldn't last long. There were too many people who needed to hear this: that God doesn't want to get involved in your life just to ruin it.

He wants to show you how to make it happen.

Chapter Nine

But God wasn't finished wowing me yet.
Not by a long shot.

After thirty-six years of life, I finally began to live. Even though I was still broke and barely eking out a living at the gym and at a part-time job, I was a published author now. What else could matter? So what if I have to buy food at a dollar store and pay my rent in installments?

I'm published.

The editor at HarperCollins was wonderful. She and I hit it off perfectly and worked well together. For me, this was just another confirmation of God's intervention—like the moment I noticed the company's logo was a flame of fire over water—both signs of the Holy Spirit. Now what were the odds of that happening?

For a while after this first happened, every time I prayed I cried, and I mean cried until I was bawling my eyes out. I was just so deeply grateful. No one had ever helped me like this before, and especially not when I really needed it. Every time I thought about what God did for me, it was like a dam bursting inside me, and I'd just lie there weeping for joy.

No one could have been more wrong about God than me. When this all began, I was convinced that God was a cold disciplinarian whose only followers were oddballs and Jesus freaks. I had no idea he was so kind, so intimately interested in me and my dreams and my seemingly inconsequential little life. This was a God who got involved, not to restrict, but to free. He let me soar to heights I could only dream about before.

And he did it all with the most tender, thoughtful, almost

romantic kind of love. No wonder I was now singing all the love songs on the radio to God rather than to some imaginary man who never materialized.

"I want to know what love is, and I want you to show me."

"Bring me a higher love."

"I never knew there was a love like this before."

"Here I stand with my everlasting love."

And nothing was more thrilling than the way he began to put all the pieces together for me, showing me how he had been at work in my life from the very start.

Like how the dream of writing came upon me at Penn State at the same time that I received a strong impulse to return to Mass. I suddenly realized that the call to write had come from God. I took the gift but refused the giver. What touched me the most was that he could have taken it back, but he allowed me to keep it, knowing that the dream of becoming a writer would become like a lifeline for me when my world turned black. This is what I clung to when my marriage fell apart and my heart was broken, when I lost my job and was so terrifyingly poor.

Never in a million years did it occur to me that this dream of mine came from God. But how could I doubt it after the events of the last year? For fourteen years I tried to be published, but to no avail. It wasn't until I turned back to the Giver that it finally happened.

My dream was his dream! I still remember the night this truth first sunk it's profound little claws into my heart. I thought of all the bliss I experienced whenever I escaped into the limitless horizons of a novel, allowed myself to get lost in the characters, the plot, the imagined sensations and emotions. It was like living in a parallel universe—just the thing I needed when life was too hard, too unforgiving. Even though I had rejected him, pushed him away, he didn't take his gift back the way a conditional lover would do. He gave all that to me, just because he loved me.

But God wasn't finished wowing me yet. Not by a long shot.

I'll never forget the day my books arrived—all twenty-five complimentary copies. I tore open the box and held a book in my hands like it was coated in twenty-four carats.

The cover was exquisite, in romantic shades of blue. And there was my name at the bottom. *My name!*

That night, I decided to take a trip with the Lord to the nearest mall where the two of us could share that exhilarating moment when I would see my book on a bookshelf for the first time. The closest bookstore was a Waldenbooks. I headed straight for the fiction aisle and there it was, midway up the shelf, wedged between rows of other titles.

It was like the miracle was happening all over again. After all those years of unrequited effort, seeing my book on the shelf was like watching the Red Sea part in front of me. Naturally I pulled out two of my books and placed them on the shelf with the covers showing.

"Can I help you with anything?" the sales clerk asked.

I smiled. "That's my book!" I said cheerily. "And I want everyone to see it."

"Oh, how nice," she said and looked at me like I was some kind of nut-job.

"Seriously...I'm the author!" I insisted but she was backing out of the aisle now, nodding her head and trying not to look like she was afraid of me. OK, so I don't look much like a published author in my jeans, sneakers and "My Indian Name Is Runs-With-Beer" sweatshirt.

My parents were very interested in reading my book, but I was

very nervous about it. What if they didn't like it? I was especially
worried because there was a love story in the book where the characters consummated their love. Surely Mom would be mortified
when she read this. The last thing I wanted to do was make them
feel ashamed.

But there was no way to prevent my mother from reading a book
published by one of her own children.

I gave her a copy.

After three days of my suffering repeated bouts of diarrhea,
she finally called.

"I can't put it down!"

My heart skipped a beat.

"What?"

"Your book! It's the best story I ever read! I can't believe you
wrote it!"

Thanks, Mom.

"But what about the sex?"

"Oh, it's so tastefully written I would let even the younger ones
read it."

Now I know there's a God.

I didn't have a bad day for a whole year. It was a time to discover
life all over again—life absent the constant struggle to achieve a
dream. Now it was time to enjoy its fulfillment, and I savored every
moment of it.

True to his usual generous self, the Lord tucked a myriad miracles
into all the nooks and crannies of my fabulous year. Like the night
I was flipping through my Bible and came across the date of July
23—the same day that my great miracle occurred. It was in the
book of Esther, which is the story of a beautiful Hebrew woman
who became the beloved queen of a non-Hebrew king. She never

told the king, or anyone else for that matter, that she was a Jew. An evil member of the king's court hated the Jews and eventually persuaded the king to issue an edict commanding that all the Jews were to be killed. When Esther heard this, she finally went to the king and revealed the truth about herself, risking death to save her people. But the king loved her so much, he commanded that the edict be rescinded, thus sparing the lives of the Jews.

The date of the reversal of that edict was July 23. This was the same day the Lord chose to make my dream come true. But I knew that with God, there are no coincidences. He picked this day for a reason. Was it the reversal of my own eternal death sentence, the one I so richly deserved because of the way I had been living?

Even more intriguing was that the biblical Queen Esther is said to symbolize the role the Mother of God plays in the lives of Christians. Could this mean that it was Mary who had pleaded for my soul and won for me the grace of conversion? But how could this be when I never once prayed to her, I wondered, even though the answer came before the question was fully raised.

Unconditional love.

From that day on, I have been devoted to Mary.

But then God decided I needed another dazzling exposition of his power. Although it certainly didn't feel like it, perhaps there was still some element of doubt in me that there really was a God, and that he had worked this great miracle in my life. Or maybe my cake just needed a little bit more icing.

I had just finished revising another one of my novels and sent it to Gerry for consideration by HarperCollins. Gerry kept warning me that second novels were notoriously difficult to place, especially when a writer's first book had not been out long enough to prove itself in sales. Those warnings went in one ear and out the other.

Who cares what happens to everyone else's second book? I'm with God, and he can do anything.

All my attention was focused on the one-year anniversary of my happy day—July 23—and I planned a nice big dinner for me and him and time spent together in prayer. As usual, I came home from work, kicked off my shoes and hit the flashing red button on the answering machine exactly as I had done the year before.

"Sue, this is Gerry. You better call me right away. Harper just made you an offer, and I think you should take it."

For a moment, I just stood there as still as stone.

Did I just hear what I think I heard?

I hit the button again.

"Sue, this is Gerry. You better call me right away."

Good Lord! He did it again—and on the *exact same day* as last year. The odds against that happening have to be astronomical!

"OK, Lord," I said out loud. "If I didn't believe before, I sure do now! You really got me this time!"

It was true, and I never knew it as keenly as I did later that night when I flipped open my Bible to a page in the second chapter of Song of Songs that only he could have picked:

"Arise, my love, my fair one, and come away; for now the winter is past, the rain is over and gone. The flowers appear on the earth; the time of singing has come...."

Epilogue

Trust me, God will either part your "Red Sea"
or give you something better, because
that's just the way our Creator is.

I always wanted to write my love story with God, and I guess you can say this is the first installment. What you just read is only the beginning of what became one of the most unexpected and thrilling journeys of my life.

But that's the subject of another book—or two.

I am now the author of six books (this is number six, and a seventh is in the works). All have been published, and none have made me more than pocket change, but the fulfillment factor makes it all worthwhile.

In addition, I'm employed full-time as a writer, just as the Lord predicted.

"One day you will write for your life," he would tell me over and over again in the way he usually "talks" to me, which is more like a sudden influx of knowledge than the actual hearing of words. But being the "doubting Thomas" that I am, I didn't believe him and chalked it up to my infamous imagination. Every time he said it, I hoped with all my might that it was true but would usually quip something like, "Will that be before or after death, Lord?"

I was soon to learn that once God enters your life, there's no such thing as coincidence anymore. It's all part of his plan.

For instance, I thought he was just keeping me busy exploring the spiritual side of life when my rather unconventional way of praying led me into the deeper realms of contemplative prayer.

The girl who used to quip sarcastically, "What do I look like, a Carmelite?" became a fully professed lay member of the Discalced Carmelites in the year 2000.

During the formation program, while studying the works of the great Carmelite mystics such as Saint Teresa of Ávila and Saint John of the Cross, I was inspired to write pamphlets about prayer that my pastor allowed me to put in the literature rack in my parish.

This was where an acquaintance of mine, who had just become the editor of our diocesan newspaper, picked one up, read it and liked it. Not long afterward, she came up to me after a meeting and said, "You know, Sue, I'm looking for a writer, someone who knows something about prayer. I've noticed the pamphlets you write, and I hear you've had some novels published. Would you want to give it a try?"

"But I don't know anything about writing for a newspaper," I argued.

"If you can write a novel, you can write for a newspaper," she insisted.

She hired me as a reporter, even though the only thing I knew about reporting was what I saw on the nightly news.

"Just go out and buy a tape recorder," my dad reassured me. "Tape everything you hear, then come home and type it up. Nothing to it!" Spoken like a veteran reporter—except that he's an engineer/physicist.

I took his advice, bought the recorder, and hurried out to cover my first event: a protest at an abortion clinic. I got lost on the way, my new car stalled in the middle of the busiest exit ramp on the Pennsylvania Turnpike, and I was so nervous my blouse was sticking to my back by the time I arrived. But arrive I did, flipped on the recorder, and started my career in journalism.

Compared to writing 250,000-word novels, writing a 500-word article turned out to be a piece of cake. I started cranking out articles on prayer, spirituality, and every social issue you can think of from abortion to euthanasia and embryonic stem-cell research. I loved it!

Within a year, I started winning awards left and right. Every time I turned around I was getting another one. People started inviting me to speak in their parish. They took my picture and wanted my autograph. For the longest time, I would just look at them in amazement and wonder, "Is this really happening to me?"

After a five-year stint as a reporter for a diocesan newspaper, I went to work as a staff journalist for Johnnette Benkovic of EWTN's *Women of Grace*. Her dynamic apostolate could not be more perfectly suited to a reformed feminist like myself. Its whole purpose is to educate women about what the Church calls authentic femininity—essentially what is contained in that brilliant document that so changed my way of thinking about God, the Church, and women: *Mulieris Dignitatum*. How perfect is that?

On the personal side, David's God and I continued our romance, which deepened and became so precious and satisfying that I one day realized the idea of getting married wasn't so thrilling anymore. Once you find a "higher love," there's no going back.

Needless to say, by the time God got done with me (and from what he tells me, he's not finished yet), my puny little dream of becoming a writer seemed more like a TV sitcom compared to a full-length motion picture. No matter what I hoped for, he outdid it in spades. Naturally I started liking his way much better than mine.

Looking back on it now, I can see that until God came along, I was a person trapped in a life that just didn't fit. Even though I excelled in office work, I never felt comfortable there. I could sell anything to anybody, but I never really *liked* it. It was just a job, something I did for a living. It wasn't me.

But then God stretched out his hand and parted the "Red Sea" that was standing between my dream and me. Once I had a book in print, I blossomed from the inside out. For the first time in my life, I was comfortable in my own skin. In a little more than a year, he took me from a downtrodden, never-had-any-luck-to-speak-of girl who always felt like the laughingstock of the family into someone who finally felt like somebody. And there I was, wasting all that time worrying about him making me into someone I'm not—like a Jesus freak—and all the while he was arranging things so that I could finally be who I am.

That's who God is, and that's the point of this whole book. It's not really about who I am but about who he is, an exquisitely polite, profoundly personal, and painstakingly present God. Forget the gargoyle. He doesn't exist. The real God is the ultimate gentleman, especially with reluctant modern girls like me, and is careful never to impose himself where he has not been invited. He respects our freedom, and that very behavior from him is what makes a person feel so dignified, so worthy.

And so, when you come to that "Red Sea" in your life, that seemingly impossible hurdle that you desperately want to surmount, allow me to recommend David's God, the good old-fashioned God of Abraham and Isaac. Trust me, he'll either part your "Red Sea" or give you something better, because that's just the way our Creator is.

After all, he's been there and done that.

And if he can do it for me, he can do it for you.

About the Author

Susan Brinkmann, OCDS, author and award-winning journalist, is a member of the Third Order of Discalced Carmelites (secular). She is the staff journalist for *Women of Grace*, she authors the *Breaking News* and *New Age Q&A* blog for the ministry, and she's a frequent guest on EWTN's *Women of Grace* television show with Johnnette Benkovic. Susan Brinkmann also authored *The Kinsey Corruption* (Ascension Press 2004) and *Learn to Discern: Is it Christian or New Age?* (Simon Peter Press 2008).